Butterflies

By Eric Braun and Sandra Donovan

Raintree

ANIMALS OF THE RAINFOREST

www.raintreepublishers.co.uk

Visit our website to find out more information about Raintree books.

To order:
☎ Phone 44 (0) 1865 888112
🖹 Send a fax to 44 (0) 1865 314091
🖥 Visit the Raintree Bookshop at www.raintreepublishers.co.uk to browse our catalogue and order online.

First published in Great Britain by Raintree Publishers, Halley Court, Jordan Hill, Oxford, OX2 8EJ, part of Harcourt Education.
Raintree is a registered trademark of Harcourt Education Ltd.

Originated by Dot Gradations Ltd
Printed and bound in Hong Kong and China by South China

ISBN 1 844 21106 1
07 06 05 04 03

British Library Cataloguing in Publication Data
Braun, Eric
Butterflies - (Animals or the rainforest)
1. Butterflies - Juvenile Literature
2. Rainforest ecology - Juvenile Literature
I.Title 595.7'8
A catalogue for this book is available from the British Library.

Acknowledgements
The publishers would like to thank the following for permission to reproduce photographs:
Ahmad M. Abdalla, p. **15**; Digital Stock, pp. **28–29**; Hemera/Photo Objects pp. **5**, **9**; Photo Network/Kevin Caldwell, p. **1**; Richard Cummings, p. **6**; Root Resources/ C. Postmus, pp. **8**, **20** (all photos on page); Earl L. Kubis, pp. **19**, **26** (right); Tony Rath Photography, pp. **16**, **22**; Visuals Unlimited/A. Kerstitch, p. **11**; Bill Beatty, p. **12**; Fritz Pölking, p. **24**; Kjell Sandved, p. **26** (left).

Cover photograph by Fogden Wildlife Photographs.

Every effort has been made to contact copyright holders of any material reproduced in this book. Any omissions will be rectified in subsequent printings if notice is given to the publishers.

Contents

Any words appearing in the text in bold, **like this**, are explained in the Glossary.

Range of the
blue morpho butterfly

Surrounding land

Sea

Borders

Rivers

A quick look at butterflies

What do butterflies look like?
Butterflies come in many different colours and sizes. They have four wings, two on each side of their bodies.

Where do butterflies live?
Butterflies live all over the world, except near the North and South Poles. Most live in tropical places. The rainforests of Central and South America have more kinds of butterflies than anywhere else.

What do butterflies eat?
Butterflies only eat liquids. Usually, they eat nectar. Nectar is a sweet liquid found in plants and flowers. Some also feed on the juices of animals and waste. Many butterflies do not have to drink water. They get enough liquid from the nectar they drink.

Unlike other insects, butterflies taste and smell with their feet.

Butterflies in rainforests

Many insects, such as dragonflies, have lived on the Earth for 300 million years. The first butterflies appeared only about 120 million years ago. One scientific name for butterflies is Lepidoptera (lep-uh-DOP-tur-uh). The name comes from words that describe a butterfly's wings.

Butterflies are insects, like ants and beetles. An insect is an animal that has six legs and a body that is divided into three parts. The parts are the head, **thorax** and **abdomen**. The thorax is between the head and the abdomen. The stomach is in the abdomen. Most insects also have wings.

▲ This caterpillar will undergo metamorphosis to turn into a butterfly.

Metamorphosis

Butterflies start as **caterpillars**. Caterpillars look like worms. They have soft bodies and short, stumpy legs. They do not have wings.

After several weeks or months, caterpillars start to change into butterflies. This change is called **metamorphosis**.

Butterflies live all over the world except near the North and South Poles. They love the sun and are more common in warm parts of the world. Some places have more butterfly species than others. The small country of Costa Rica in Central America has many different kinds of butterflies. In fact, it has more butterfly species than all of Africa.

Role in the rainforest

Butterflies have an important job in the rainforest. As they fly from one flowering plant to another, they brush against pollen on the plants. Pollen is a powdery material that plants make so new plants can grow.

Butterflies **pollinate**, or spread pollen, each time they visit a flower. By pollinating plants, butterflies make more plants grow. Without butterflies, there would be fewer flowering plants. Without flowering plants, there would be fewer butterflies.

Types of rainforest butterfly

There are more than 28,000 different species of butterfly. A species is a group of animals or plants most closely related to each other. Most butterflies live in tropical places. These are hot and rainy areas of the world. Many are found in rainforests. Rainforests are warm places where a lot of rain falls. Many different kinds of trees and plants grow close together there.

Butterflies come in many different colours. Ulysses butterflies have bright blue wings. They live in the rainforests of Australia. They are sometimes called mountain blue butterflies. Zebra Longwing butterflies have yellow stripes on their black wings. They live in the rainforests of Central and South America.

Butterflies also come in different sizes. Some have a wingspan as large as a dinner plate. An animal's wingspan is the distance between the tips of its wings. One kind of butterfly called the Queen Alexandra's birdwing butterfly has a wingspan of more than 28 centimetres. The smallest butterfly is the western pygmy blue. Its wingspan is only 15 millimetres.

This long-winged zebra butterfly is looking for food in a flower.

Some butterflies fly very fast, and others are very slow. Monarch butterflies fly up to 27 kilometres (17 miles) per hour over long distances. Skipper butterflies are even faster, flying at up to 48 kilometres (30 miles) per hour. They cannot fly very far at this speed. When they fly, they start and stop, start and stop and start and stop again and again.

These butterflies are puddling. This means they are drinking water from wet sand.

Where butterflies live

Butterflies live all over the world, except near the North and South Poles. They live where they can find the best climate and food to stay healthy. They also live where they are safest. The tropical rainforests of Central and South America have the most butterflies.

Butterflies use rainforest plants for shelter from the weather and also to hide from **predators**. Predators are animals that hunt other animals and eat them. The safest places for butterflies to sleep are under leaves or between cracks in rocks.

Groups of butterflies often rest in sunny spots. They need the heat and energy from the sun to warm their bodies. Their bodies must be warm to be able to fly. Some butterflies will spread their wings to soak up the sun's heat. This is called basking.

Groups of butterflies will also gather at wet or muddy spots on the ground. This is called puddling. They drink the water at these spots.

Many butterflies spend their whole lives in one place. Others travel great distances. They move with the seasons to find the best food and weather. This kind of travel is called migration.

Monarch butterflies migrate the furthest. In the autumn, large groups of monarchs fly from North America to Central and South America. They have also been found in Australia, Hawaii and on other islands in the Pacific Ocean.

Appearance

A butterfly's head includes its eyes and **proboscis**. The proboscis is part of the mouth. When it is not being used, the proboscis is rolled up under the butterfly's head. The head also has **antennae**, or feelers. Butterflies use their antennae to smell and to keep their balance when they fly.

Butterflies have four wings, two on each side of their thoraxes. Each species has different wing markings and colours. Some butterflies have colours that blend in with their habitats. A habitat is a place where an animal or plant usually lives. Shapes, patterns and colours that help things blend into the background are called camouflage.

Kinds of wings

The monarch butterfly's wings are bright orange with black lines and borders. This helps predators, such as birds and lizards, tell monarchs apart from other species. They leave monarchs alone because they taste bad.

Morpho butterflies have large blue wings. The undersides of their wings have spots. The spots look like eyes. They are called eye spots, and they fool predators. A bird aims for a butterfly's head.

▲ **The spots on the underside of this morpho butterfly's wings protect it.**

If it is fooled by the eye spots, it strikes the butterfly's wings instead. This usually does not hurt the butterfly, and the butterfly escapes.

When a butterfly with large eye spots spreads its wings, it can look like a predator itself. One butterfly with large eye spots is the owl butterfly. When it spreads its wings, the eye spots look like an owl's eyes.

This butterfly is drinking nectar from the flower.

What butterflies eat

Caterpillars and butterflies eat different kinds of food. Caterpillars eat small parts of plants, such as leaves. They have hard mouth parts for eating tough plant leaves. Caterpillars need to eat plants to grow into butterflies.

Once caterpillars change into butterflies, they do not eat any solid food. They need only liquid food, such as nectar. Nectar is a sweet liquid found in plants. Usually, butterflies eat only nectar from flowers. Some butterflies, however, also feed on the juices of dead animals and waste. Many butterflies do not have to drink water. They get enough liquid from the nectar they drink.

How butterflies eat

Because butterflies do not eat solid food, they never need to bite or chew. Most insects have jaws, but butterflies do not. Instead of biting they use their proboscises. These work like straws to suck up liquid food. Butterflies unroll their proboscises and use them to find nectar deep inside flowers. Then they suck up the nectar. They have a special pump in their bodies called a cybarial pump. This helps them suck.

How butterflies find food

The first thing many caterpillars eat is the egg case from which they hatched. Usually, caterpillars hatch on the plants that will be their food. They use their short legs to climb around the plant to eat small parts of the leaves.

Caterpillars eat to stay healthy and to change into butterflies. Once they are butterflies and have wings, they fly from plant to plant.

Butterflies can see well, and this helps them find food. They can see the bright colours of flowers. They can also see some colours that people cannot see. These colours show butterflies where nectar is.

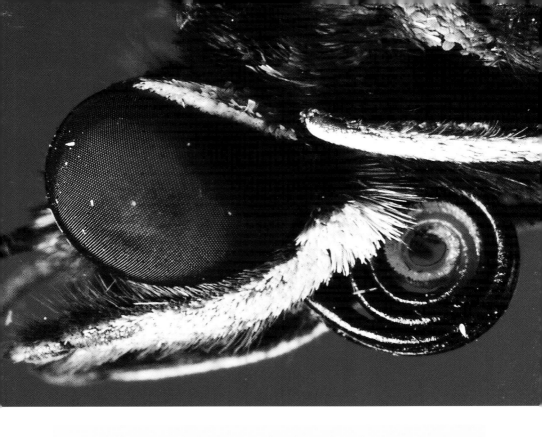

▲ **This butterfly has its proboscis rolled up under its head.**

A butterfly's feet also help it to find food. When it lands on a plant or flower, its feet can sense wetness. This tells the butterfly if the plant has nectar to eat. Butterflies have a very good sense of smell. They smell through their feet and their antennae. Their sense of smell also helps them find flowers with nectar.

The metamorphosis of a butterfly

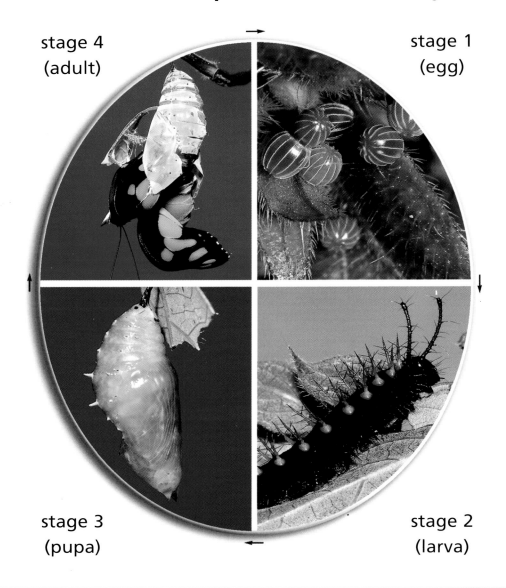

stage 4
(adult)

stage 1
(egg)

stage 3
(pupa)

stage 2
(larva)

A butterfly's life cycle

Butterflies pass through four stages in their lives. The stages are the egg, the **larva**, or caterpillar, the **pupa** and the **adult**, or butterfly.

Butterfly eggs hatch into caterpillars. Caterpillars have a head, a thorax and an abdomen. They have thirteen body sections and several legs. All caterpillars can spin silk threads.

Caterpillars eat leaves and gradually grow larger. They moult, or shed their skin for new skin, as they grow. After a few weeks or months, they attach themselves to a leaf or a branch. They moult one last time. This time, under the skin is a **chrysalis** or cocoon. It becomes hard. Inside the chrysalis, the caterpillar becomes a pupa.

The pupa slowly goes through a process called metamorphosis. Metamorphosis means a change in form.

This butterfly is crawling out of its chrysalis.

Pupa to adult

The pupa changes into an adult butterfly. It grows legs, wings and antennae. The change may take from a few days to two years.

After metamorphosis, the skin of the pupa splits open. Then the adult butterfly crawls out. After only a few hours, it is ready to fly away.

Most butterflies live for only a few days or weeks. Because their lives are short, they look for a mate immediately.

Usually, males travel in groups to look for females. Sometimes they gather on one plant and wait.

Butterflies mate only with butterflies of the same species. They can tell if another butterfly is the same species by its colours and patterns.

Butterflies also use their sense of smell to find mates. Females have a special scent that attracts males. Males will sometimes follow a scent for long distances. Once a male finds a female, he releases a scent, too. It usually comes from his wings or abdomen.

Laying eggs

Female butterflies usually lay their eggs in the summer, soon after mating. Butterflies usually lay eggs on the undersides of plant leaves. The eggs are often green to blend in with the leaves.

Females usually lay many eggs at once. This is because a lot of the eggs will be eaten by other animals before they can hatch. The more eggs a female lays, the better their chances of hatching.

Butterflies need trees and plants to live in.
They can die without their habitat.

Butterflies in the world today

There are not as many butterflies now as there were a few years ago. About fifty species of butterflies are endangered around the world. Endangered means that the whole species could die out if things are not done to protect them and their habitats.

People are the biggest danger to butterflies. People are cutting down trees in the rainforests to build roads and buildings. They are clearing land to grow crops and farm animals. They also sell the wood from the trees. Many animals in the rainforests, including butterflies, are losing their habitat.

Butterfly   Moth

Here are some of the differences between a butterfly and a moth.

Time of activity
Most butterflies fly during the day.

Most moths fly at night.

Appearance
Butterflies are usually brightly coloured.

Moths usually have dull colours.

Antennae
Butterflies have knobbed antennae that look like lollipops.

Moths have antennae that are often straight, feathery or branched.

Wings when at rest
Butterflies usually fold their wings together.

Moths rest with their wings open.

Future of butterflies

Some people collect butterflies. Hunters capture and kill butterflies, and then sell them. Collectors display the dead butterflies for other people to see.

Butterflies are also having a harder time finding host plants. Host plants are plants that butterflies need for food, for places to sleep and for laying eggs. These plants live in the rainforests that are being destroyed.

Some people are trying to save butterflies. They work to save their homes and host plants. They try to teach others about how important butterflies are to flowering plants. These people know that learning about butterflies is one of the best ways to save them. Together, people can use what they learn to help keep butterflies alive in their rainforest homes.

antennae
see pages 14, 19

proboscis
see pages 14, 18

legs and feet
see page 19

colourful wings
see page 14

abdomen
see page 7

Glossary

abdomen back part of an insect's body

adult final stage of an insect's development

antennae feelers on the head of an insect

caterpillar (KAT-ur-pil-ur) worm-like larva stage in a butterfly's life cycle

chrysalis (KRIS-o-lis) hard case that protects a caterpillar while it turns into a butterfly

larva early stage of an insect's development, such as the caterpillar stage in a butterfly's life cycle

metamorphosis changes in an insect, such as a butterfly, as it develops from an egg into an adult

pollinate to spread pollen so that new plants can grow

predator animal that hunts other animals to eat

proboscis straw-like mouth part that animals use to suck up liquids

pupa stage of an insect's development just before it becomes an adult

thorax middle part of an insect's body between its head and abdomen

Internet sites

London Butterfly House
www.butterflies.org.uk

World Wide Fund for Nature (WWF)
www.panda.org

Useful address

WWF-UK
Panda House, Weyside Park
Godalming, Surrey
GU7 1XR

Books to read

Hartley, K; Macro, C. *Bug books: Caterpillar.*
Heinemann Library, Oxford, 1999

Royston, Angela. *Life Cycle of a Butterfly.*
Heinemann Library, Oxford, 1999

Index